KEYSTONE STATE RAILS

MODERN RAILROADING IN WESTERN PENNSYLVANIA

MATTHEW V. CRAFT

FONTHILL

Fonthill Media Inc.
www.fonthillmedia.com
office@fonthillmedia.com

First published 2024

ISBN 978-1-62545-143-9

Typeset in 10pt on 13pt Sabon
Printed and bound in England

Contents

About the Author

Born and raised in Western Pennsylvania, Matthew Vincent Craft is an award-winning photographer. In college he discovered a love for photography, continuing to develop and hone the skill after school while living on the West Coast. Upon returning to Pennsylvania, he traveled across the Keystone State and documented the unique and challenging railroading operations of the region. When not photographing railroads, Matthew also focuses on landscape, wildlife, weather, and astrophotography.

www.mattcraftphotography.com

Introduction and Acknowledgments

Pennsylvania has long been a keystone in America's rail network, and few states can match it in terms of freight volume or railroad heritage. Pennsylvania's dense rail network is largely built upon four major trunk lines (Pennsylvania Railroad, Baltimore & Ohio Railroad, New York Central Railroad, and Erie Railroad) that crossed the state at the turn of the twentieth century. These lines have changed hands several times over the following century, ultimately evolving into a modern freight network that serves as a corridor, moving a significant volume of the freight that passes between the east coast and the rest of the nation. In addition to this through freight, Pennsylvania also generates a significant amount of originating tonnage thanks to the state's productive coal, oil, and agricultural markets, as well as the prodigious industrial output from both sides of the state (Pittsburgh and Philadelphia). There are few states that can match the volume of freight that passes through Pennsylvania, but what makes railroading in the Keystone State truly fascinating is the varied and challenging terrain that these railroads conquer every day.

It was apparent early on in this project that one could write a book devoted solely to each of the mainlines that weave across Pennsylvania. While this book will highlight some of the most prominent and iconic railroading locations across the western half of the state, it would be impossible to fit them all within these pages. To that end, if there is a personal favorite location that you feel was overlooked and could have been featured in the pages to come, I would love to learn of it, and can be reached at *mattcraftphotography@gmail.com*

I could not have created this work without the assistance of a number of local experts, notably Chad Lilly (*HistoricBF* on YouTube), Wallie Bednarsky (*WallieB26* on YouTube), and Dave Cole (*ccrx6700* on YouTube). These men have been invaluable resources in the research and writing of this book, in addition to providing excellent company while trackside. Thank you all for your help. Additionally, I would like to thank Chris Johnston, both for his role in encouraging me to pick up a camera again and for accompanying me on a significant number of the road-trips spent gathering images for this book. Thank you for making those trips more fun than they would have been otherwise. I would be remiss if I didn't acknowledge my family; I would like to thank my mother and father, Timothy and Rosemary, as well as my sisters Stephanie, Andrea, and Kimberly, my brother-in-law Matthew, and my niece, Juniper. Thank you all for the constant encouragement throughout the duration of this project. Stephanie, thank you for your help with the preparation of this manuscript. Lastly, I would like to thank my friends. I truly appreciate your encouragement and critique over the past two years, and I can say with certainty that this project would not have happened without it.

1
CSX

The CSX Corporation was created in 1980, born out of a merger between Seaboard Coast Line Industries and Chessie System, Inc. The two holding companies owned and operated a number of railroads, notably the Baltimore & Ohio Railroad and Western Maryland Railways. CSX Corporation was initially a holding company, but in 1987 the merger was finalized and CSX Transportation as we know it today came into existence. In 1998, CSX acquired 42% of Conrail's assets (with Norfolk Southern purchasing the rest), adding nearly 3,600 miles of track (most of it former New York Central routes) to its rail network overnight. CSX currently operates a rail network of over 20,000 miles, spanning the entire east coast between Florida and Quebec, and running as far west as the Mississippi River.

CSX has long referred to itself as a "triangular network," having established three freight corridors: the I-90 Corridor at the top (connecting Chicago, IL to Selkirk, NY), the I-95 Corridor on the right (connecting Selkirk to Jacksonville, FL), and the Southeastern Corridor on the left (connecting Chicago to Jacksonville). One part of the triangle runs through Pennsylvania; the I-90 Corridor traces along the shore of Lake Erie through Northwestern Pennsylvania. Additionally, CSX's I-95 Corridor is fed via the former B&O mainline that runs through Western Pennsylvania (upgraded in 2011 to allow for expedited double-stack container traffic between Chicago and the East Coast ports).

CSX runs a blend of both new and rebuilt motive power. The days of a healthy mix of Electro-Motive-Diesel (EMD) and General Electric (GE) power are long gone, with CSX running almost exclusively GE power (mostly GEVOs, though there are still plenty of AC4400s and Dash 8s in service) on its road trains. That doesn't mean that CSX has entirely abandoned EMD; there are still a large number of GP38-2, GP40-2, and SD40-2 locomotives performing yard duties and providing power for local trains. Like the GE engines, these old EMD workhorses have undergone extensive updates and rebuilds through the years.

CSX's Erie West Subdivision is the portion of the I-90 Corridor that runs through Northwestern Pennsylvania. The Erie West Subdivision is roughly 45 miles of double-tracked mainline, running through Pennsylvania from border to border. This former New York Central route follows the shores of Lake Erie through the State Game Land forests in the west and on through the vineyards in the east. Due to the relatively non-existant grade and long stretches of straight track that define this route, trains are able to travel at up to 60 mph across most of Pennsylvania. The Erie West Subdivision is CSX's busiest line in Pennsylvania, serving as the company's main artery between Chicago and New York City. More freight tonnage traverses these rails than anywhere else in CSX's Pennsylvania network. In addition to the freight traffic, Amtrak's *Lake Shore Limited* (an overnight passenger service that runs between Chicago and both Boston and New York City) travels across this route. This busy mainline parallels Norfolk Southern's Lake Erie District, a former Nickel Plate Road mainline, throughout the entirety of Pennsylvania. There are long sections of track where the two main lines are separated by only 80 feet, setting the stage for frequent meets and the opportunity to witness CSX and NS trains racing one another. The regional weather can be a factor for rail traffic both in the summer and the winter months given this route's proximity to Lake Erie. Severe summer storms can move in off the lake at a moment's notice and impose temporary slow orders, and lake effect snow squalls can blanket the entire region under a deep layer of snow. Erie averages between 7-8 feet of snow each winter, and a lake effect storm can paralyze the region. For context, the Erie Airport recorded an astonishing 34 inches of snow in a single lake effect storm event in 2017. To say that it is challenging to keep the mainline open and passable in these conditions would be an understatement.

CSX's I-95 corridor is fed via the former B&O mainline that runs through Western Pennsylvania, crossing the border with Ohio in Robinson, PA. From there, the New Castle Subdivision (originally a Pittsburgh & Lake Erie route that B&O operated via trackage rights) runs approximately 9.5 miles alongside the Mahoning River until reaching the town it was named after, New Castle. The New Castle Subdivision terminates at the south end of the CSX New Castle Yard in West Pittsburg. This is also the spot where the P&W Subdivision interchanges with the New Castle Yard. While CSX once owned this right of way, they leased (and eventually sold) it off to the Buffalo & Pittsburgh Railroad (BPRR) and the Allegheny Valley Railroad (AVR). The BPRR exchanges rail cars with CSX daily in the New Castle Yard.

The CSX Pittsburgh Subdivision begins after the P&W Junction. This former P&LE mainline turns south and follows the Beaver River through Wampum and Beaver Falls. The mainline crosses the Ohio River in Beaver and turns east, continuing on through to Pittsburgh. Trains frequently stop at the Pittsburgh Holdout (located at the base of the Duquesne Incline) to wait for westbound traffic to clear a single-tracked tunnel in Pittsburgh's South Side. Once cleared east, rail traffic passes through the tunnel before continuing on to Homestead and past the sprawling shopping plazas that have replaced the steel mills that this city was once known for. The Pittsburgh Subdivision ends in McKeesport, just beyond where the mainline turns east to follow the Youghiogheny River.

This marks the beginning of CSX's Keystone Subdivision, a well-known former B&O route that features the notorious Sand Patch, a challenging mountain grade. CSX operates a small classification yard in Connellsville. Amtrak also has a station at the western end of the yard, served daily by their *Capitol Limited* passenger train that runs between Washington, D.C., and Chicago. The mainline continues east from here, climbing gradually alongside the Youghiogheny River (a popular whitewater rafting waterway) through Ohiopyle State Park and on through to the town of Confluence. To this point, the mainline has been double-tracked, but those tracks split in Confluence. The No. 1 main (the "High Line") features a steep 1.2% grade, but a shorter overall distance traveled; the No. 2 main has a ruling grade of just 0.7% but is an additional 2.3 miles of distance traveled when the two tracks rejoin after the Brook Tunnel.

Continuing east from this point, the Keystone Subdivision has changed greatly over the past decade. In 2013, CSX completed their National Gateway project, a multi-year, multi-state project that increased freight capacity on the former B&O line by increasing the clearance in many of its tunnels, and in several cases by removing the tunnels altogether in a process called "daylighting." The Shoo Fly, Pinkerton, and Benford Tunnels were all deemed easier to remove as opposed to undergoing complex clearance-lengthening construction projects. This has allowed for this route to serve as an artery for double-stacked traffic to and from Chicago, feeding CSX's I-95 corridor and East Coast ports. The Keystone Subdivision continues east alongside the Casselman River, taking advantage of the gentle slope of this water-level route on through to the town of Meyersdale. The grade sharply increases at this point to 1.5%, the steepest section of track on the west slope. It is 8 miles until the summit of the Keystone Subdivision, and eastbound trains often slow to a crawl as they battle against the incline of the mountain. The mainline crests the top of the Allegheny Mountains, passing through the small town of Sand Patch at an altitude of 2,258 ft. The summit of the Keystone Subdivision is commemorated with a concrete elevation marker planted trackside.

As trains crest the summit and start heading down the east slope, they enter the Sand Patch Tunnel, a 4,475-foot double-tracked tunnel that passes 234 feet below the Allegheny Mountains. Trains exiting the eastern portal emerge out into the Chesapeake Bay Watershed and immediately embark across the steepest portion of the Keystone Subdivision. The grade down from Sand Patch to the small town of Mance is a steep 1.94%, and while it does slightly ease as the mainline runs through the town of Glencoe, it will remain a steep and challenging obstacle until it reaches the town of Hyndman. After navigating around the scenic horseshoe bend in Mance, the mainline follows alongside Wills Creek all the way to the border of Pennsylvania and Maryland. While this waterway looks tame, the creek has flooded several times over the years, its waters rising the 30 feet up and over the right-of-way and washing the mainline out. Flash floods are just one of the weather-related challenges inherent to mountain railroading; the area also is prone to heavy snowfalls in the winter. The isolated and inaccessible nature of large swaths of this route add to the challenge of keeping it open throughout the winter.

The steepness of the east slope is evident when comparing the distances traveled to the corresponding elevation gain against that of the west slope. The west slope traverses nearly 70 miles of terrain between Connellsville and Sand Patch, gaining almost 1,300 feet in elevation; the east slope by comparison covers a distance of roughly 35 miles between Sand Patch and Cumberland but gains nearly 1,600 feet in elevation. The steep grade on the east slope proves a challenge to freight trains even in this modern era; it is not uncommon for westbound trains climbing the grade out of Cumberland to stall out and require assistance up and over the mountain.

A New York bound intermodal train enters Pennsylvania at track speed, ripping past the Canadian National Conneaut Yard at 60 mph. You can see the now-unused yard lead that once connected the former Bessermer & Lake Erie Railroad yard to the mainline running behind the signals.

A westbound double-stack train rolls through a slow order (a temporary speed restriction, in this case due to the presence of severe thunderstorms). The weather in this region can be quite volatile given the mainline's proximity with Lake Erie, both in the summer and winter months.

A Canadian Pacific intermodal train whips up a small blizzard as it rolls through North Springfield, PA. CP has a "Haulage Rights" agreement with CSX that allows CP trains to run across CSX territory (with the foreign equipment being run by CSX crews).

An overview of the GE Transportation (now a part of Wabtec) manufacturing facility in Erie, PA. These shops are the point of assembly for many of the GE Evolution Series locomotives. Additionally, Wabtec offers repair/rebuild/modernization services that can significantly extend the service life of older locomotives.

The lineup of locomotives awaiting rebuilding in Erie. This holding area can feature some very interesting and colorful power, such as the Massachusetts Bay Transportation Authority F40PH-2C's in the foreground. The GE/Wabtec facility connects to both the CSX and NS mainlines that run behind this yard (you can see a CSX manifest rolling east towards New York in the background).

An eastbound manifest train sits on Main 2 while a higher priority intermodal train passes by on the adjacent track before it switches back over to Main 2 in North East, PA.

A CSX container train highballs through mile after mile of the Lake Erie Grape Belt (the second largest grape growing region in the U.S.). The CSX Erie West Subdivision and the Norfolk Southern Lake Erie District run parallel to each other from border to border, but between Erie and North East the two mainlines are separated by only 80 feet.

A westbound manifest train passes underneath the rickety Bort Rd. bridge as it crosses the NY border and heads towards North East, PA. The NS mainline turns away here as it approaches Twenty Mile Creek, but it will rejoin the CSX trackage again in New York.

An eastbound CSX mixed freight crosses into Pennsylvania as it traces alongside the Mahoning River toward New Castle, PA. The New Castle Subdivision terminates approximately 9.5 miles further east, in New Castle, PA.

Eastbound trains must cross the Shenango River just prior to entering the CSX New Castle Yard limit. The original B&O right-of-way had substantially more trackage than you will find these days, evidenced by the empty spans that once supported tracks. This empty coal train is running east on Main 2, which will bypass the yard entirely.

A westbound loaded coal train departs from the New Castle Yard and accelerates towards the PA/OH border. CSX frequently utilizes Distributed Power Units (or DPUs) to improve train handling and to allow the railroad to run longer, heavier trains. These DPUs are remotely controlled engines that are spaced throughout the train; in this case this single DPU is pushing on the rear of the heavy coal train as it leaves the yard.

Kasgro Rail Corporation is connected to the north end of the New Castle Yard. This is the home of the world's largest rail car, KRL 3601. This monstrosity is a Schnabel car (a specialized rail car that carries oversized and overweight loads in such a way that the load becomes a structural part of the car) that was designed to carry nuclear reactor pressure vessels. The car has a total of thirty-six axles (eighteen on each half) which distributes the weight of the load over a larger area of track.

It is not uncommon for trains entering CSX's New Castle Yard to stop and collect a fresh crew before continuing their trip. CSX 454 (the "Spirit of Magnolia" heritage unit) sits at the head of a westbound intermodal train awaiting a new crew. The yard has had a number of tracks removed over the years, resulting in the much more spacious arrangement in place today.

A pair of GEVO's assemble a train in front of a lineup of former Union Pacific Genset locomotives. These locomotives are likely on their way to a nearby scrap yard in Lordstown, OH.

New Castle Yard is bustling with activity on a cold December afternoon. Two CSX westbound trains (the intermodal and coal trains) are stopped and waiting for fresh crews, while another CSX freight manifest assembles their train in the yard. While all this is happening, a colorful set of Buffalo & Pittsburgh Railroad light power is slowly rolling through the yard on their way to shut down for the day.

CSX 1973 sits tied down in West Pittsburg, a frequent crew change stop for eastbound traffic. This locomotive is the second heritage unit that CSX has painted with a special livery that pays homage to the railroads that once ran down these tracks, in this case the famous Chessie System.

The crew for the autorack in the background ties their train down while an eastbound manifest freight rolls out of the yard on Main 3 before crossing over to Main 1 at the P&W Junction. This is where the BPRR's P&W Subdivision connects with CSX's New Castle Yard.

The Chessie System heritage unit is on the move! After receiving a fresh crew, CSX 1973 picks up speed, barely beating an approaching thunderstorm as it heads south toward Pittsburgh on Main 2.

CSX 1973 rolls through Wampum, PA, accelerating to track speed (50mph on this section of mainline) after clearing the New Castle Yard. The CSX Pittsburgh Subdivision passes underneath Norfolk Southern's Youngstown Line in Wampum.

The Beaver Bridge crosses over the Ohio River in Beaver, PA. This bridge has been in service for over 100 years, originally carrying P&LE and B&O rail traffic across the river.

Just past Neville Island is a staging yard that holds empty covered hoppers for the Shell ethylene cracker plant 20 miles down the Ohio River. The plant produces polyethylene pellets, which are loaded onto the hoppers and shipped across the country. There is also a transload facility on-site, which allows for the transfer from covered hopper railcars to trucks for final delivery for any non-rail-served industries.

A short frac sand train with a Union Pacific leader rolls through McKees Rocks, PA. This staging yard occupies the same land where a short-lived (2017–2020) intermodal facility once stood.

The Pittsburgh Subdivision crosses underneath the Pittsburgh and Ohio Central industrial lead that descends to the Ohio River and on to the POHC/CSX interchange further west near Neville Island.

The Pittsburgh Holdout is a frequent stopping point for eastbound trains. The double trackage ends 2.5 miles ahead, just prior to the J&L Tunnel (which runs underneath a portion of Pittsburgh's South Side). It is not uncommon to see a train stopped here, waiting for a westbound train to clear the tunnel.

A rebuilt GP40-3 sits at the Pittsburgh Holdout across the Ohio River from the Carnegie Science Center (and the WWII submarine, USS *Requin*) and the Acrisure Stadium (home of the Pittsburgh Steelers). This unit was originally built as a GP40 that served the B&O Railroad in the 1970s; CSX updated these units in the 2010s with new cabs, electronic handbrakes, an auto start, positive train control, and a new traction control system.

An eastbound loaded coal train sits in the Pittsburgh Holdout on a hot summer evening, waiting for three westbounds to clear the J&L Tunnel before getting underway again. The streak of light is the headlight and numberboards from a passing intermodal train.

The Homestead Stacks tower over the CSX Subdivision, a memorial to the Homestead Works steel mills that have long since been replaced by a sprawling shopping center. These twelve stacks once vented the 45" Slab Mill, which closed in 1986.

CSX 412 throttles up as it heads out over the Monongahela River and across Pinkerton's Landing Bridge. In the background stands the iconic Carrie Furnace, one of the only preserved blast furnaces from Pittsburgh's famed steel industry. The lead unit shares the number "412" with the Pittsburgh Area Code, and it was fitting to photograph it in front of such an important piece of Pittsburgh's history.

A loaded autorack train heads out over the P&LE McKeesport bridge and across the Youghiogheny River (the river that these tracks will run alongside for the next 65 miles). The third track leads to the CSX Mon Subdivision, which interchanges with Norfolk Southern in Brownsville and gives CSX access to the coal mines in Southwestern Pennsylvania.

If you get lucky you can occasionally find CSX trains on NS rails. These CSX coal trains are operated by NS crews while on the Manor Branch. The NS crew will load the train at the Bailey Mine loader before traversing back down the Manor Branch and the Mon Line. The train will be handed off back to the CSX crews in Brownsville, PA.

Some of the coal trains that load at the Bailey Mine complex originate from western railroads that interchange with CSX and then run their trains down CSX lines (thanks to trackage/haulage rights) to pick up a fresh load of Pennsylvania coal. This KCSM "Grey Ghost" leader is a rarity on these rails.

An eastbound autorack train departs CSX's Connellsville Yard, passing underneath the expansive signal bridge that covers all six tracks leading into the yard. Connellsville was once a hump yard, but the hump has long been removed in these days of Precision Scheduled Railroading. Connellsville receives a fraction of the traffic it did back in the B&O days.

It is not uncommon to see intermodal trains with no double-stacks run down the Keystone Sub, such as this one near Confluence, PA. Trains running to Philadelphia from Cumberland must deal with low clearances along their route and the current solution is to run intermodal trains with only single-stack containers. CSX is actively working on increasing clearances along their Interstate 95 transportation corridor, so these single-stacked container trains will soon be a thing of the past.

An intermodal train charges uphill on Main 1 through Confluence, PA. The town was named Confluence because it is the meeting point of the Casselman River, Laurel Hill Creek, and the Youghiogheny River.

A westbound container train descends down the "High Line," deep in the dynamic brakes. The rail is slick after a short-lived thunderstorm, so extra care is required when descending the steep grade. The mainline splits apart in Confluence; Main 2 (the "Low Line," which deviates to the right) was built as a lighter-grade alternative to the High Line.

An autorack train runs up the Low Line through Harnedsville, PA. This portion of the route traces the Casselman River and provides an easier grade for heavy eastbound trains. The expense of this lesser grade is an extra 2.5 miles of distance.

Railroads frequently transport oversized loads, such as this transformer. This train was heading west towards Connellsville, but the yard called ahead and informed the crew that they would not be able to accept a high and wide car and instructed them to set the car out at GARRETT before continuing their journey.

The power from a train of Herzog ballast hoppers (the observant will note the fresh ballast laid over the center tracks) detaches from its train and heads out onto the mainline at GARRETT. Now that the ballast cars are empty, these engines will run around and connect to the other end of the train before heading back to Cumberland.

Having reversed down the length of their train, the engines slow as they prepare to couple to the cut of empty ballast cars. This train will sit in the siding between the signals at YODER and GARRETT until a fresh crew can be driven out to take it back to Cumberland.

The sun has passed below the horizon as this manifest freight rolls down the 1.5% grade west of Meyersale and over the crossovers at YODER. Traffic had just started flowing again after a westbound autorack train had stalled in the Sand Patch Tunnel for several hours in the afternoon.

An intermodal train roars underneath the Salisbury Viaduct (a former Western Maryland Railway bridge that is now part of the Great Allegheny Passage hiking trail) in notch 8 (the highest throttle setting). The grade sharply increases for eastbound traffic just before Meyersdale, PA, which slows heavier trains considerably.

A pair of cyclists traveling the Great Allegheny Passage stop on the Keystone Viaduct to watch an eastbound intermodal thunder up the steepest part of the west slope.

An eastbound intermodal train rounds the bend at the summit of the Sand Patch grade. You can hear eastbound traffic, engines bellowing and echoing through the valleys, coming for as much as ten to fifteen minutes before the train crawls around the bend.

A westbound autorack train climbs up and over the summit of the Keystone Subdivision in Sand Patch, PA. It's all downhill from here for westbound traffic heading towards Pittsburgh.

The Sand Patch Tunnel was widened in the early 2010s to allow for double-stack traffic to transit the Keystone Subdivision. A westbound double-stack train takes advantage of those upgrades as it pulls through the west portal of the tunnel and approaches Sand Patch, PA.

After summiting the Alleghenies and passing through Sand Patch Tunnel, eastbound trains have to be quick on the brakes as they start down the East Slope. A combined autorack/intermodal train snakes down the steep 1.94% grade just before entering the curve at Mance, PA. This is the steepest grade on the Keystone Subdivision.

Altoona isn't the only location in Pennsylvania with a horseshoe curve. While not as world-famous as its Norfolk Southern counterpart, CSX's Mance Curve is every bit as renowned by local photographers and railfans alike. In this image, a westbound container train pulls hard uphill and around the bend in front of the old Mance Post Office.

A manifest train heads downgrade and around the Mance curve. This is the point where the old B&O right-of-way meets Wills Creek, which it will follow for the next 25 miles until the PA/MD state line.

Looking east from Mance, you can see the mainline following the contour cut into the ridge by Wills Creek. The sandstone and quartzite that form the backbone of the Allegheny Mountains is exposed where the mountain was cut into (the fill of which was used to backfill and create the Mance curve).

An intermodal train passes an autorack train just east of the Foley Overlook. One can see just how inaccessible parts of the Keystone Subdivision can be out in the Allegheny Mountains and understand why it can be so challenging to keep this route passable in the winter.

A westbound autorack train passes through the Falls Cut Tunnel. This tunnel was constructed in 1897 and rendered a sharp curve that followed the contour of Wills Creek obsolete.

A mid-train DPU crosses Wills Creek on Main 1 before entering the east portal of the Falls Cut Tunnel. The original B&O mainline curved to the right and out the bottom of the frame before the tunnel was built.

The Keystone Subdivision snakes through the Allegheny Front, running between two parallel ridges: Little Savage Mountain to the north (left) and Big Savage Mountain to the south (right).

An intermodal train is barely making 10 mph as it grinds up the notorious Sand Patch grade through Fairhope, PA. Wills Creek runs alongside the right-of-way. While it appears peaceful here, this valley is prone to flash floods and the creek has swelled in excess of 30 feet to wash out the mainline in the past.

The mainline crosses Wills Creek one last time before exiting Pennsylvania. This container train is running south toward Cumberland on Main 2, coasting down the last bit of downhill grade before the Cumberland Yard.

An autorack train heads north across the Pennsylvanian border and through Cooks Mill, PA. The grade here is relatively shallow, which, coupled with the straight run of track, allows for 50 mph running.

2

Norfolk Southern

The Norfolk Southern Railroad was, as is often the case, born out of a merger. In the summer of 1982, the Norfolk and Western Railway and the Southern Railway consolidated to form Norfolk Southern. NS had sought to purchase Conrail in 1985, but the two companies would not merge until 1998, when NS was able to secure the right to purchase 58% of Conrail's assets (CSX purchased the remaining 42%). The Conrail split added 7,200 miles of track to the NS network, most of it former PRR routes (with the crowning gem being PRR's "Main Line," the fallen flag's primary route across Pennsylvania). At the time of this writing, NS operates 21,300 miles of trackage, stretching up and down the east coast from Florida to New York, and as far west as Kansas City. The former PRR "Main Line" is among the busiest rail routes on the east coast.

When compared to CSX, Norfolk Southern operates a much more diverse fleet of locomotive power, with a healthy mix of both EMD and GE engines on the roster. One of the major windfalls of the Conrail acquisition was the Juniata Locomotive Shop complex in Altoona, PA. This extremely capable and versatile repair facility was founded by the PRR in the 1850s. While the shop's reputation was established in the steam era, a modernization program in the 1950s transitioned the shop into a premier diesel locomotive repair/rebuild facility. The shop complex is as busy as ever at the time of this writing; modernization and rebuilding programs make upgrading existing locomotives to current standards more cost effective than buying brand new motive power outright. One significant rebuild program of note resulted in the creation of the SD40E, which were famously used in manned helper service (where additional locomotives are coupled to a heavy train and used to help push it over a grade) on the Allegheny Mountains. These locomotives were custom designed in-house by Juniata engineers, built on the frames of retired EMD SD50s and equipped with the prime mover from a SD40-2. There were also cab improvements and upgrades, including the addition of in-cab signaling (a requirement for any unit leading a train on the Pittsburgh Line) and Helperlink (which allows helper units to disconnect on the fly). These units typically operated in "four-packs," though it was not uncommon to see a pair of SD40Es pulling on the head-end of a train with another four pushing on the rear. The SD40E was removed from helper service in 2020, replaced by the SD70ACU (a rebuilt SD90MAC). These locomotives are very similar to the SD70ACe, though they still retain the look of the massive SD90MAC. NS upgraded the units with in-cab signaling and Helperlink, in addition to increasing the overall weight of the locomotive (slightly improving the tractive effort the engine is capable of delivering). Each unit delivers 4,500 horsepower (compared to the SD40E's 3,000 hp) which allows them to operate in "two-packs." The NS Pittsburgh Line operates the largest pool of helper locomotives in North America. Helper crews are based out of Altoona and Johnstown, though they can travel as far as Pittsburgh.

Westbound rail traffic enters Pennsylvania on the Fort Wayne Line, a double-tracked mainline that connects Fort Wayne/Chicago to Pittsburgh. This is a vital intermodal corridor for the railroad, connecting Chicago with Norfolk Southern's East Coast intermodal terminals. The Fort Wayne Line passes through several small towns on the 25-mile run to Conway, PA. Conway was once the largest rail yard in the world (it was surpassed in size by Union Pacific's Bailey Yard in 1980). Conway is a hump yard; at the heart of the yard is an artificial hill that leads down to the classification yard. Rail cars are sorted when they are uncoupled and released to roll down the hill and automatically switched onto the appropriate classification track. Gravity does all the work here; there are retarders (mechanical brakes installed in the tracks that grip the sides of the wheels and provide braking action) in place if it is necessary to slow the cars as they roll down the hump. Conway at one time had two hump yards in service—one for eastbound traffic, one for westbound. In 2002, the eastbound hump was closed and the retarders and classification tracks were removed, leaving just the westbound hump to service the entire yard. Continuing east from Conway, the Fort Wayne Line follows the contour of the Ohio River all the way to Pittsburgh.

Things become complex as the mainline approaches the Steel City. The route expands from three tracks to six about 4.5 miles west of the city, two of which diverge from the Fort Wayne Line and cross the Ohio River on the 1.5-mile-long Ohio Connecting Bridge. This marks the beginning of the Mon Line. The tracks expand again along the north shore of the Ohio River and into the NS Island Avenue Yard, continuing down the Fort Wayne Line. This yard was once a busy TOFC (Trailer on Flatcar) terminal, but that changed in the 1990s when Conrail repurposed the Pitcairn Yard in East Pittsburgh for intermodal operations. Since then, Conrail (and now, Norfolk Southern) has used this yard primarily for locals (trains that deliver or pick up cars from the railroad's customers, as opposed to through-freights that shuttle those cars from yard-to-yard) and for interchanging freight with other railroads. The eastern end of the yard narrows to four tracks that pass through the Allegheny Commons Park utilizing a feature famously known as "the Trench." These four sunken tracks will split apart just past the park into two mainlines. The two middle tracks will continue west alongside the Allegheny River and become the Conemaugh Line. This low-clearance mainline traces the banks of the Allegheny, Conemaugh, and Kiskiminetas rivers. The longer, circuitous route makes for a much more manageable grade profile, which allows for heavy coal/ethanol/manifest trains to make it further east before requiring the addition of helper engines. The Conemaugh Line reconnects with the Pittsburgh Line at the CONPIT Junction just west of Johnstown, allowing for smoother overall operations on the Pittsburgh Line.

Heading back to Pittsburgh, the two outside tracks exiting "the Trench" ramp up and over the Conemaugh Line and across the Fort Wayne Bridge in downtown Pittsburgh. This marks the end of the Fort Wayne Line and the start of the Pittsburgh Line. The tracks round the bend and enter the Pittsburgh Union Station, which is served by *The Pennsylvanian* (a daily passenger service connecting Pittsburgh and New York City via Philadelphia, primarily utilizing NS trackage) and by the *Capitol Limited* (a daily passenger service that runs between Washington, D.C., and Chicago, primarily on CSX trackage). This portion of the Pittsburgh Line has clearance issues which limits the height of rail cars that are able to pass through downtown Pittsburgh and on to East Pittsburgh. The Turtle Creek Valley is a choke point for rail traffic; both the NS Pittsburgh Line, the NS Port Perry Branch, and the famous Union Railroad mainline run through this valley. The Port Perry Branch was originally built by the PRR to relieve rail traffic congestion around Pittsburgh by allowing through-freights to bypass the city; these days it is used to connect the Pittsburgh Line to the Mon Line. This is Norfolk Southern's only high-clearance route through Pittsburgh, and every double-stack intermodal train that passes between Chicago and Harrisburg will be routed across the Ohio Connecting Bridge, down the Mon Line, and through Pittsburgh's South Side before crossing the Monongahela River on the Port Perry Bridge and ultimately ending up on the Pittsburgh Line. This won't be the case forever; at the time of this writing, NS has untaken several projects around Pittsburgh to raise the clearances of a number of bridges and other low-clearance obstacles along the Pittsburgh Line. One day soon, double-stacked containers will roll through downtown Pittsburgh and through "the Trench."

The Mon Line continues alongside its namesake, the Monongahela River, to the NS Shire Oaks Yard. This part of the Mon Line is primarily a coal artery that connects the southwestern Pennsylvania coal mines to the larger U.S. rail network. As such, Shire Oaks is used as a staging yard for coal trains. Empty coal trains will continue south from here, on through to Waynesburg, where the Mon Line ends, and the NS Manor Branch begins. This branch line was built in 1984 during the Conrail era, the tracks weaving uphill through the remote Pennsylvanian backcountry to the Bailey Mine Complex. The line ends with the track looping back on itself at the Prep Plant and train loadout facility. There are three mines (Bailey, Enlow Fork, and Harvey) that send coal to the Prep Plant via a sprawling, miles-long network of conveyor belts. Once at the prep plant, the coal is washed and crushed to a uniform size (dictated by the customer) before being loaded onto a train for delivery. The loadout facility is capable of loading up to ten unit trains a day, and they load trains around the clock.

Picking back up with the Pittsburgh Line, the former PRR Pittsburgh Division trackage passes through the towns of Greensburg and Latrobe before running into the first of many serious obstacles: the western face of the Allegheny Mountains. The mainline turns north and parallels the contour of the mountain until it reaches Torrance. The Conemaugh Line rejoins the Pittsburgh Line here (albeit on the opposite side of the Conemaugh River), and both mainlines turn east and enter the Packsaddle Gap. They will run side-by-side for approximately 8 miles until reaching the CONPIT Junction, where the Conemaugh Line ends. The Pittsburgh Line is a triple-tracked mainline from this point on to Altoona, with Main 1 primarily being used for eastbound traffic and Main 3 being used for westbound. The middle track, Main 2, is used for bidirectional traffic depending on the situation. The three tracks continue southeast along both sides of the river until reaching Johnstown. This is the primary helper base for the western slope, and it is not uncommon to see several pairs of SD70ACU helpers sitting in East

Conemaugh, waiting on their next assignment.

This spot marks the beginning of what is colloquially known as "the Mountain." The 40 miles of triple-tracked mainline running between Johnstown and Altoona climb up and over the Eastern Continental Divide, summiting the Allegheny Mountains in the town of Gallitzin. The west slope (between Johnstown and Gallitzin) is the easier of the two grades. It takes nearly 30 miles to climb the west slope; comparatively it only takes 10 miles to climb to the same altitude if starting out on the east slope. The Pittsburgh Line passes through several well-known railfanning locations, including the Cassandra Overlook (an old bridge that crosses the mainline and provides an excellent photography platform) and the town of Cresson (the RJ Corman shortline interchanges with NS in this mountain town). The Pittsburgh Line reaches the summit of the Allegheny Mountains 2 miles further east, in the town of Gallitzin. The mainline splits apart here, with Mains 2 and 3 diverging to the north and through the heart of Gallitzin before entering the Allegheny Tunnel, while Main 1 continues straight ahead before entering the New Portage Tunnel. These tunnels mark the beginning of the eastern slope; trains heading to Altoona and onward must smoothly transition from pulling their train up and over the mountain to managing a tricky descent down the steepest, most challenging portion of the mainline. Mains 2 and 3 exit the Allegheny Tunnel on a 1.7% grade, while Main 1 descends a steep 2.46% grade known as "the Slide." Main 1 is primarily used for eastbound traffic (as many westbound trains simply would be unable to climb the steep grade). The three tracks rejoin at Bennington Curve (the site of a PRR passenger train derailment in 1947). The mainline mirrors the contour of the mountain as trains wind down past the MG Interlocking (while the tower is still there, it is no longer in use and inaccessible) before reaching the world-famous Horseshoe Curve.

The Horseshoe Curve is a marvel of engineering that is without question the most famous railroad landmark in America. Laid out by PRR Chief Engineer J. Edgar Thomson in 1850, this sweeping 220 curve was the railroad's solution to reducing the steepness of the east slope as it neared the summit of the Alleghenies. Construction began with laborers cutting into the hillside of Kittanning Point and filling in the ravines on either side to create the right-of-way. The curve was opened four years later, with a total project cost of $2.5 million. Heavily promoted by the PRR, the Horseshoe Curve became a popular tourist destination, bolstered by the National Park Service declaring the site a National Historic Landmark in 1967. There is a park at the top of the hill where you can watch the trains grind around the bend from trackside, as well as a visitor center at the base of the mountain.

The 1.74% ruling grade continues from the Horseshoe Curve and along the next 4 miles of mainline until reaching the base of the "the Mountain" in Altoona, PA. Amtrak operates a station in downtown Altoona, visited twice every day by *The Pennsylvanian*. NS still operates a small yard here across from the massive Altoona Works complex (the east end of which is the Juniata Locomotive Shop). Rose Yard isn't much more than a crew change point and helper base these days, a far cry from the busy hub that it was in years past. Opposite the yard and across the mainline lay the storage tracks for the Juniata Shops, filled with around 100 different locomotives in various states of disrepair. Some of these locomotives will be scrapped, some will be scoured for parts, but most will be rebuilt and upgraded. The Pittsburgh Line continues east past Altoona, following the Juniata River on through to Harrisburg (though this book will only cover as far west as Altoona).

Norfolk Southern also operates another mainline through Pennsylvania in the northwestern part of the state. The Lake Erie District of NS is a part of the former Nickel Plate Road mainline, which stretches between Buffalo and Chicago alongside the Great Lake it was named after. It was formerly a part of the Cleveland District, but the route was split apart, the portion from Buffalo to East Cleveland being the Lake Erie District, and the portion from Cleveland to Bellevue being the Cleveland District. This route is not as heavily traveled as the NS Pittsburgh Line, and only sees a fraction of the traffic of the CSX Erie West Subdivision, which runs parallel the Lake Erie District from Ohio to New York.

A Norfolk Southern manifest train belches smoke as it throttles up, moments from crossing the border into Ohio. The setting sun reflects off the heads of the rails as they round the bend west of McRoberts Crossing.

Operating a railroad is an inherently risky endeavor, and the public was explosively reminded of that fact on a frigid night in Feb 2023 when fifty-one cars of a NS manifest train derailed in East Palestine, OH (on the border of PA). Unfortunately, eleven of the cars involved were carrying hazardous materials and the explosive venting and subsequent cleanup have been quite controversial.

An eastbound intermodal train passes a stopped manifest freight train in Enon Valley, PA. This long exposure shot was taken six months after the East Palestine derailment and only one track had reopened, which is why this mixed freight train is waiting for the intermodal train to pass before continuing west.

Fresh snow blows off the covered hoppers as this train accelerates up to track speed after stopping in Conway Yard to receive a fresh crew. The two cement pillars once supported a pair of signals before the control point was moved down the road to Enon Valley.

The "Barcode Unit" (NS 1111) rounds the bend in the Highland Cut, past another recent derailment. This is the highest point of the Fort Wayne Line, and it is not uncommon to find heavy trains stalled out in the cut.

A NS manifest train passes underneath Interstate 376 as it crests the peak of the Fort Wayne Line and coasts downhill into Conway Yard. There is no shortage of farmland nor pastures trackside along this stretch of the line.

A LORAM rail grinder approaches the Highland Crossing as it rolls through Big Beaver, PA. You can see the sparks flying as this interesting piece of equiptment grinds off any excess wear and restores the profile of the railhead, extending the life of the rail.

A westbound intermodal with a GEVO leader kicks up a trackside snow squall as the engineer sounds their horn for the Highland Crossing. NS has an in-cab signal requirement for the Fort Wayne Line, which is why it is extremely rare to find anything other than a NS unit leading a train.

A container train emerges out of a band of snow, trying to pick up speed on the icy climb out of Conway. The train has just cleared the crossovers at CP WOOD after passing through Homewood, PA.

The NS Heritage Unit that honors the fallen Savannah & Atlanta Railroad (NS 1065) is at the head of a westbound intermodal train, cutting through the rain in Big Beaver, PA. The heritage locomotives pay homage to railroads that played significant roles in Norfolk Southern's history.

A loaded double coal train (200 cars in a 2x2x2 power arrangement) heads out over the Beaver River in New Brighton, PA. The NS Fort Wayne Line crosses over the CSX Pittsburgh Subdivision on the west side of the span.

A manifest train slowly passes underneath the Fort Wayne Line. The mainline splits on the east side of the Beaver River Bridge and Main 2 crosses over the NS Youngstown Line, which will merge with the Fort Wayne Line a mile south at CP BRIGHT.

A high priority intermodal train on Main 2 speeds by a freight manifest that's stopped on the Youngstown Line, waiting for a signal to proceed into Conway Yard. You can see the slope of the Youngstown Line, dropping down to pass underneath the Fort Wayne Line.

A container/piggyback train speeds past a stopped manifest freight in New Brighton, PA. The CSX Pittsburgh Subdivision runs parallel to the Fort Wayne Line across the Beaver River. This area can be a bit of a choke point for rail traffic on both sides of the river; it is not uncommon to find trains stopped here, waiting for other traffic to pass.

Looking south past CP BRIGHT is another example of the bottleneck around Conway Yard, this time for westbound traffic. An ethanol train (with some Canadian foreign power behind the NS SD70ACU) sits and waits for the eastbound intermodal train to come through the control point before getting underway again.

A Conway-bound manifest train crosses over the confluence of the Beaver and Ohio Rivers, slowly rolling down the end of the NS Cleveland Line before entering the Conway Yard. While the Cleveland Line usually only has a couple trains each day, NS was forced to rely on it more heavily while the Fort Wayne Line was closed after the East Palestine derailment.

Norfolk Southern's Conway Yard was once the largest rail yard in the world, and while its footprint has been reduced over the years in the name of efficiency, this hump yard is still a bustling hub of activity. In this shot, two different westbound manifest trains are being assembled (one of which has the Conrail Heritage Unit, NS 8098, at the head end).

A springtime shower washes over the east end of the yard, with a faint rainbow leading down to the hump. This view shows just how large the yard is, even with its modern reduced footprint.

NS 8098 pulls the first half of its train out of the yard. Once it is clear, the conductor will throw the necessary switches and the train will reverse and couple to the mid-train DPU and the remainder of its train.

A bird's-eye view of the old turntable and the engine servicing facilities at Conway Yard. The service tracks around this area are always very busy, and the tracks around the turntable are usually full of locomotives in various states of disrepair.

Another angle of the trackage around the Conway Locomotive Shop, as well as both humps and the westbound classification bowl. In 2002, the eastbound hump (the one in the background of this image) was closed and the retarders and classification tracks were removed. Only the westbound hump remains in operation today.

Conway Yard is always a busy location. In this frame, an ethanol train reverses deeper into the yard, the BNSF/CP mid-train DPUs for an inbound freight manifest sit idle (having just been parked and uncoupled from), a yard power set containing an engine and two slugs (additional traction motors that are powered by the head-end engine) reverses to collect the next cut of cars that will go over the hump, and in the background a local slowly approaches the eastern end of the yard.

A westbound intermodal train stops for a quick top-off and a fresh crew just outside the engine facility. Sometimes it is less time consuming to drive a fuel truck over to the train and refuel it on the mainline instead of disconnecting the engines and running them through to the servicing tracks.

The light reflecting off the rails highlights the interesting track arrangement leading into Conway. A single Dash-9 quietly rolls out of the yard, its headlights dimmed to avoid blinding the crews sitting on the three inbound trains parked on the mainline behind the cameraman, waiting for their clearance to enter the yard.

An eastbound container train departs East Conway, crossing over onto Main 3 of the Fort Wayne Line on a blustery winter day. There are two eastbound manifests making up their trains in the yard that will soon be following this intermodal train east.

A pair of Dash-9's, their noses frosted over, lead a westbound intermodal train through East Conway on a frigid March afternoon. It is not uncommon to see two to three trains pile up behind this signal bridge, awaiting clearance into or around the yard.

The conductor for a westbound manifest train climbs down and walks back the length of his train, his flashlight leaving a ghostly light trail behind in this long exposure shot. The crew was trying to get underway but was unable to release the air brakes, and the conductor had to walk back and look over each car to troubleshoot the issue.

The Norfolk & Western Heritage Unit (NS 8103) rolls through Haysville, leading a short intermodal train west towards Pittsburgh. This train was short enough that it only needed two engines to tackle "the Mountain," with the second engine being configured as a DPU further back in the consist.

A local heads to Conway through Glenfield, PA, with one of the NS Operation Lifesaver units in the lead. This train has an interesting power line-up, featuring (from front-to-back) a GP59E, an EMD Road Slug (drawing power from the lead engine), and a SD40E (formerly of the Altoona helper-pool).

A freight manifest rolls by the Island Avenue Yard office at 20 mph down Main 2. After passing through the yard, this train will continue out the Conemaugh Line. In the background, the daily AVR local that interchanges with NS picks up the cars returning to the AVR Glenwood Yard on Main 3.

The Fort Wayne Bridge that crosses the Allegheny River in downtown Pittsburgh marks the end of the Fort Wayne Line. Construction of this double-deck bridge started in 1901 by the Pennsylvania Railroad; the lower deck was taken out of service in the 1980s during the Conrail era.

Right: It's neck and neck as two boats race down the Ohio River and under Norfolk Southern's Ohio Connecting Bridge. Originally constructed in 1915, this massive double-tracked bridge is almost 1.5 miles long (including the ramp to reach the bridge's 68-foot water-clearance) and connects the Mon Line with the Fort Wayne Line.

Below: While a thick blanket of fog is a common occurrence on the river, this haze was far more insidious. June 2023 saw a thick blanket of smoke inundate much of the northeast U.S., originating from wildfires burning in Canada. An intermodal train emerges from the smoke, headed down the ramp to join with the Fort Wayne Line.

A container train crosses the northern truss of the Ohio Connecting Bridge (being the longer of the two trusses at 508 feet), heading west toward Chicago. The smoke from the wildfires gives this image an ethereal feel as the sun sets behind the haze.

The Ohio Connecting Bridge's southern end has a sharp curve, which can be unforgiving if a train is improperly built or mishandled. In April 2023, five cars were pulled off the rails in a stringline derailment. RJ Corman crews (seen here re-railing a steel coil car) responded quickly and had the Mon Line back in service that afternoon.

The derailment caused considerable congestion on the Mon Line. Every double-stack container train that passes through Pittsburgh travels the Mon Line due to clearance issues on the Pittsburgh Line. With the derailment closing both mainlines, all intermodal traffic paused on the Fort Wayne, Mon, and Pittsburgh Lines until the tracks were back in service.

The Mon Line traces the contour of Mount Washington as it passes through Station Square and under the Duquesne Incline. This funicular has been in operation for nearly 150 years, shuttling passengers/cargo between Station Square and the top of Mount Washington.

An empty coal train rolls underneath the signal bridge across from Whemco Steel Castings. The CSX Pittsburgh Subdivision (seen on the other side of the Whemco building) runs parallel to Norfolk Southern's Mon Line through Homestead, PA.

A westbound container train snakes through Homestead. The third track (seen on the left) is a running track that leads to the small yard past Homestead where NS interchanges cars with the Union Railroad.

Both Norfolk Southern and the Union Railroad operate parallel bridges across the Monongahela River in Port Perry, PA. Both bridges have a wye on the southern shore, with the URR tracks crossing over the NS trackage.

The Turtle Creek Valley below the Westinghouse Bridge in East Pittsburgh is a chokepoint for NS; every intermodal train that passes through Pittsburgh must travel both the Port Perry Branch and the Mon Line due to clearance issues on the Pittsburgh Line. At the time of writing, multiple projects are underway to raise the low-clearance obstacles along the route so that double-stack trains can avoid this bottleneck.

The Illinois Terminal Heritage Unit (NS 1072) is running as a mid-train DPU on a long 200-car empty coal train, crossing over from Main 1 to Main 2 of the Mon Line as it heads back to Shire Oaks Yard.

The south end of NS Shire Oaks Yard is primarily used as staging for coal trains (both empty and loaded). Road crews will drop off empty trains here and the mine crews will take them further onward to Bailey Mine for a fresh load of coal, after which they will be returned to Shire Oaks Yard, ready for delivery.

A southbound train of empty coal hoppers accelerates out of Shire Oaks Yard and past the decommissioned Mitchell Power Station in New Eagle, PA. This coal-fired power plant was retired in 2013.

The Mon Line runs down the middle of Main St in West Brownsville, PA. This might be the last place in America where you can regularly catch a unit coal train running down the street. Every train that runs between Bailey Mine and Shire Oaks Yard will pass down this roadway.

The Mon Line crosses the South Fork Ten Mile Creek in Clarksville, PA. This bridge has been in service for over 100 years, originally built by the Monongahela Railway. The trains today (such as this 200-car coal train) are longer and much heavier than the traffic this bridge originally carried, which truly is a testament to the engineering and construction from over a century ago.

An empty coal train heads down the Mon Line and past the triangular color light signals that are a holdout from the Conrail days. Much of the Mon Line (as well as the Manor Branch) has not been upgraded from the old Conrail signals to newer signal systems (unlike the rest of Norfolk Southern's PA rail network).

Two rebuilt GE locomotives (one sporting a fresh paint job) climb the hill and navigate the serpentine curves past Sycamore, PA. Despite the general downturn in coal traffic, the Bailey Mine Prep Plant still loads up to ten trains a day, and the Manor Branch is quite active.

A ballast train (one of the only non-coal trains that will travel this branch line) crests the top of the grade before entering the Enlow Running Track and looping around to head back down the Manor Branch. These ballast trains drop fresh stone that is then used to refresh the ballast underneath the tracks.

A pair of AC44C6Ms (one freshly rebuilt and repainted at Norfolk Southern's Juniata Shops) slow as they approach the mine with their load of empty coal hoppers. These locomotives are common on coal trains; their DC traction motors were replaced with AC motors (which have excellent performance at low speed with heavy trains) as a part of the rebuild process.

The climb out of the mine is steep, and loaded coal trains will often require the assistance of helper engines. These are different from DPUs in that these engines are manned by crews that will couple to the end of the train and provide the extra horsepower to push the heavy train up and over the hill before cutting off and returning to assist the next train.

The crew of this ballast train was having a difficult time with the remoteness of the Manor Branch as it approaches the Bailey Mine Prep Plant. They were having issues receiving a valid GPS position and the Herzog hoppers were not dropping the ballast in the pre-planned locations.

A 200-car double coal train finishes loading out and departs the mine. This train has a 2x2x2 power arrangement (though the manned helpers will cut off after the train starts down the grade back to the Mon Line).

An empty coal train stops to drop off the crew that will take the loaded train back down the Manor Branch. Due to the remote nature of this branch, this is usually the easiest way to transport a new crew out to their train.

The Enlow Running Track has enough space to hold a few trains in the event of a backup near the loader. The ballast train comes to a stop while a coal train finishes loading, all the while another empty coal train is following behind the ballast train, waiting for an opportunity to load.

A coal train is halfway through the loading process and has looped back around past its last car. The massive silos of the Bailey Prep Plant stand in the distance.

An empty coal train crawls around the bend before pulling through the coal loader, dwarfed by silos surrounding it. These silos contain the processed/washed coal that will end up loaded on the outbound trains.

The Bailey Mine Prep Plant sprawls across southwestern Pennsylvania. Fed by the Bailey, Enlow Fork, and Harvey mines, this is the most productive mining operation in the Northern Appalachian Basin. The long conveyor belt running across the landscape carries coal from the Enlow Fork Mine across nearly 6 miles of Pennsylvanian countryside to the prep plant.

Resuming our journey eastward from Pittsburgh, the Fort Wayne and Conemaugh Lines emerge from the Island Avenue Yard and the combined four tracks run through "the Trench." Running through the Allegheny Commons Park, both sides of the Trench are lined with Ginko trees, which make for an incredibly vibrant scene when the autumn foliage falls down onto the right-of-way.

What was once the iconic Heinz Company factory has been converted into loft apartments. An eastbound train (with a fresh load of Bailey Mine coal) rumbles through Pittsburgh and past the Heinz Lofts on the NS Conemaugh Line.

A loaded ethanol train rolls east through Etna, PA, ditch-lights cutting through the fog that is common along the Allegheny River. The Conemaugh Line is a low-grade alternative for eastbound traffic to the Pittsburgh Line, and NS typically will run their heaviest trains down this line (avoiding the need for helpers until nearly Johnstown, PA).

A NS GEVO sits on the side of Freeport Rd. after being involved in a derailment in Harmarville, PA. The train struck an off-highway dump truck that drove through a crossing, and even though the lead engine stayed upright, this trailing unit rolled onto its side.

NS 8099 (the Southern Railway Heritage Unit) struck a rockslide and derailed, rolling over on the NS Mon Line near Pittsburgh's South Side. Thankfully, the crew made it out with only minor injuries, which is a testament to the safety of modern locomotive cabs. After spending enough time sitting outside of Pitcairn to gather a coat of rust, this locomotive was moved to Altoona where it was eventually repaired, repainted, and returned to service in May 2023.

The headlight from an oncoming train casts an eerie glow from around the curve in Trafford on an unseasonably warm and foggy winter evening.

The NYC Heritage Unit roars around the bend at the head of an eastbound intermodal train. NS 1066 was the eleventh heritage unit that NS commissioned and pays homage to the New York Central Railroad.

The Penn Central Heritage Unit (NS 1073) cruises downgrade, dynamic brakes whining as they work to keep the train's speed in check. Engineers have three different braking options at their fingertips: air brakes (which control the braking action applied to the wheels of every car in the train), independent brakes (the locomotive brakes), and dynamic brakes (which work to slow the train utilizing the locomotive's traction motors).

Two SD40Es roll across an old PRR viaduct over Loyalhanna Creek before backing down the Unity industrial track in Latrobe, PA. These SD40Es once roamed "the Mountain" as the primary power for the Altoona helper pool but have since been relegated to local service now that the helper pool has been replaced by the newer SD70ACUs.

A westbound empty ethanol train sits at CP PACK, waiting for the intermodal train (passing on the left at track speed) to overtake it on Main 2, before crossing over and continuing westward.

An eastbound manifest train crosses the Bow Ridge Bridge on the NS Conemaugh Line. The viaduct that passes underneath the bridge was a former rail line that is now a part of the West Penn Trail. The Conemaugh Dam sits in the distance.

The Pennsylvanian, pictured here emerging from the Packsaddle Gap near Torrance, PA, is Amtrak's daily passenger service running between Pittsburgh and NYC (a trip that runs over 444 miles of scenic Pennsylvania countryside and averages nine hours in total). This short passenger train is pulled by a single GE GENESIS locomotive.

A coal train makes its way out across the Conemaugh River in Robinson, PA. This is where the Conemaugh Line and the Pittsburgh Line rejoin, although they run parallel for 3 miles until the CONPIT Junction.

An eastbound intermodal train roars around the large curve that leads into the CONPIT Junction and past a quintessential Pennsylvanian farmstead. In a quarter mile, the Conemaugh Line will end as it rejoins with the Pittsburgh Line.

An intermodal train speeds west, past a slow-moving coal train that is coming off of the Conemaugh Line and onto Main 3 of the Pittsburgh Line. Once known as the Sang Hollow Extension, this portion of the Pittsburgh Line separates from Mains 1 & 2 and runs down the opposite shore of the Conemaugh River until all three mainlines rejoin in Johnstown, PA.

Left: Heavy eastbound trains having just traveled the Conemaugh Line will typically stop once on the Pittsburgh Line and wait for a pair of manned helpers to assist them over the mountain. A pair of SD70ACUs slow to a crawl as they couple the rear of a stopped coal train before resuming their journey east.

Below: The Pittsburgh Line turns south and runs through the Conemaugh Gap (one of the deepest gorges in the country east of the Mississippi) just before Johnstown, PA. Main 3 (formerly the Sang Hollow Extension) runs on the opposite side of the Conemaugh River.

Cassandra, PA, is well known amongst the railfan community; the bridge and the small clearing on the opposite side of the tracks are a very popular location to watch the trains tackle the Mountain. A mid-train DPU shoves hard on a rare eastbound train on Main 3 (which is usually reserved for westbound traffic) on a frigid February morning.

The clearing in Cassandra provides an excellent view into Moshannon Curve. This westbound container train kicks up a vibrant maelstrom of fall foliage as it coasts down the Pittsburgh Line's west slope.

An intermodal train rolls through Cresson, PA, at dusk. This town is near the summit of the Eastern Continental Divide, and as such is a frequent stopping point for helpers pushing heavy trains up the Mountain.

Looking northeast, you can see the additional trackage for the helpers as well as the interchange with the RJ Corman Railroad. A stack train heads west with the black NS "Sonic Bonnet" (a rebuilt Dash-9 with a special livery) trailing the lead unit.

Continuing east past Cresson, the tracks split as they approach the town of Gallitzin. This is the summit of the Pittsburgh Line; as eastbound trains enter the tunnels under the town, they start downgrade and emerge out onto the east slope.

An eastbound loaded coal train out of Shire Oaks passes a westbound empty on its return journey to Shire Oaks. While the Pittsburgh Line may not be quite the coal conveyor belt that it once was, there is still a steady flow of coal trains over the Allegheny Mountains.

A pair of manned helpers head downhill, using their dynamic brakes to help control the speed of the westbound train as it starts to descend the west slope. It is not uncommon for the helpers to stay on after a train crests the top of the grade in order to assist with braking.

A westbound manifest train emerges from the Allegheny Tunnel on Main 3, its engineer notching the throttle back as more of the train starts to head downgrade.

A rebuilt Dash-9 roars out of the west portal of the Allegheny Tunnel underneath Gallitzin, just moments before sunset. This tunnel's clearance was increased in 1995 to allow for double-stacked container traffic.

The headlights of an approaching westbound train light up the inside of the Allegheny Tunnel, illuminating the rarely seen tunnel interior. The plaque on the left commemorates the year the tunnel was enlarged, and its 3,600-foot length.

A pair of SD70ACU helpers disappear into the eastern portal of the Allegheny Tunnel as they shove a heavy manifest freight over the summit. The gray box above and offset from the coupler is the Helper Link box that gives these locomotives the ability to disconnect from the train while it is still in motion.

East of the tunnels, Main 1 (on the right) rejoins Mains 2/3 via a steep 2.46% descending grade. Known as "the Slide," this section of track is primarily used for eastbound traffic. A westbound empty coal train is climbing toward the Allegheny Tunnel while an eastbound manifest begins to descend the east slope.

A westbound manifest freight climbs the sweeping 220-degree Horseshoe Curve, wheel flanges squealing around the observation area. Below the curve there are three reservoirs (they were quite low when this image was taken) that supply the region with water.

An eastbound manifest train juggles both its dynamic and air brakes to maintain control of the consist as it descends down the steep mountain grade and around the Horseshoe Curve.

This angle effectively illustrates the difference in elevation from when a train enters the curve compared to when it exits. It was spring in Western Pennsylvania, and the newly sprouted foliage takes on vibrant green hue on "The Mountain."

A single GEVO slowly rounds Scotch Run Curve, pulling for all it's worth up the east slope. Though the GE engine is a reliable workhorse, it alone is not enough to tackle the mountain grade, and the manifest train had to stop in Altoona for a pair of helpers to couple to the rear of the train.

Seen here departing Altoona in the late afternoon for its return leg to Pittsburgh, Amtrak's *Pennsylvanian* passes underneath CP SLOPE. This control point marks the beginning of the climb up the Mountain.

The Pennslvanian makes a scheduled stop at the Altoona Transportation Center on its way back to Pittsburgh. Across the tracks is the Railroaders Memorial Museum, which features a large collection of PRR history and is well worth the price of admission.

An aerial overview of the entire Altoona Works complex (which today is primarily the Juniata Locomotive Shop complex). Altoona itself was established by the PRR, and in 1850 construction of the shops began. These facilities have withstood the test of time, proving their worth in the age of steam, then again in the diesel era.

These days the Juniata Locomotive Shop primarily rebuilds, upgrades, and repairs locomotives. It is not uncommon to find units in various states of disrepair strewn around the facility, such as this ES44AC that has had its prime mover ripped out.

The northeast end of the facility has a turntable that is used to shuttle engines into the correct bay within the machine shop.

Three pairs of SD70ACU helpers sit in Rose Yard, waiting to be called into action for their next shove up "The Mountain." On the other side of the mainline sits the Juniata Locomotive Shop complex and the beginning of the long line of locomotives awaiting servicing.

3
Shortlines

The Keystone State has a wide variety of regional railroads and shortlines, with nearly seventy different Class II and III railroads (including a number of independent operators and heritage/tourist railroads) in operation across the state. Most of these smaller railroads operate on rail lines abandoned by Conrail and CSX. The largest of the Class II railroads operating in Pennsylvania is the Buffalo & Pittsburgh Railroad, running on over 600 miles of former CSX/Conrail lines in western Pennsylvania. Operated by Genesee & Wyoming (a shortline railroad holding company that owns over 100 different railroads across America), the BPRR operates a small rail yard and engine shop in Butler, and interchanges with NS, CSX, and a number of other shortline railroads. The R. J. Corman Railroad operates nearly 300 miles of ex-Conrail trackage in Central Pennsylvania, and primarily interchanges with NS. Another Class II railroad, the Wheeling and Lake Erie, operates on nearly 100 miles of mostly former NS lines. The WLE interchanges with NS and CSX as well as several greater-Pittsburgh area shortline railroads. These Class II railroads exchange cars with the Class I railroads such as NS and CSX for final delivery to the customer, which extends the reach of the larger railroads. Additionally, they connect with the numerous local shortlines, stretching their reach even further. For example, in 2021 an unexpected rise in the cost of natural gas resulted in the Homer City coal fired power plant being pressed back into service. This was not planned, and as a result the power plant needed to refresh its dwindling coal stockpile. It took the effort of three railroads to transport coal from the mine to the generating station; the cars were loaded on the Wheeling and Lake Erie Railroad and interchanged with the Allegheny Valley Railroad, who then interchanged the cars with the Buffalo & Pittsburgh Railroad. The BPRR went on to ultimately deliver the coal train to the power plant. It is not uncommon for rail cars to change hands between several different railroads before being delivered to the customer.

Not all Class II and III railroads operate in this manner; some are designed from the ground up to fulfill a specific purpose. That was the case with the Bessemer and Lake Erie Railroad, founded in 1897 by Andrew Carnegie with the intention of hauling iron ore from the Lake Erie port in Conneaut, OH, to the Carnegie Steel Company foundries in the Pittsburgh region. The 139-mile route from Conneaut to Penn Hills is still in operation to this day (albeit under the Canadian National flag now, with the Canadian railroad having purchased the Bessemer in 2004), providing iron ore for the Edgar Thomson Steel Works in Braddock. The services of another shortline railroad are required to move the iron ore from the North Bessemer Yard to the foundry. The Union Railroad is a Class III switching railroad that serves the United States Steel Mon Valley Works (the USS Edgar Thomson Steel Works, the USS Irvin Works, and the USS Clairton Works). The Union's switchers (the railroad operates a mix of EMD SW1500 and MP15DC switchers) service these three facilities and facilitate the steel manufacturing process.

Another interesting operation of note is the Cumberland Mine Railroad. This private carrier mining railroad (owned by Iron Senergy) operates 17 miles of track between the coal mine located near Kirby (in Southwestern Pennsylvania) and their Alicia Dock facility alongside the Monongahela River. What makes the Cumberland Mine Railroad unique is the fact that the right-of-way is completely isolated from other railroads; there are no outside connections or interchanges with the North American railroad network. This presents a challenge when the railroad is looking to take delivery of new (or replacement) locomotives and rolling stock. The remote area and its rolling hills made the prospect of transporting them via truck daunting. As a result, the decision was made to deliver the locomotives and rolling stock on the opposite bank of the Monongahela River, disassemble them, float them across the river to the Alicia Dock, and then reassemble them on the Cumberland Mine tracks.

The mine operates a total of three locomotives (one EMD SD40-2 and two SD38-2s, all of which are facing east). In an effort to streamline operations, all three locomotives were equipped with Locotrol, which allows them to be remotely operated or run as a Distributed Power Unit. Commonly referred to as a "DPU," this is when an engine is placed further back in the consist and is remotely operated from the lead engine, allowing for more precise train handling and longer overall train lengths. While the mine has the ability to operate two trains simultaneously, they typically operate just one (with between 38-40 coal hoppers that are bookended with a single SD38-2 on each end). This is peak efficiency when it comes to railroading; the Cumberland Mine Railroad is not burdened by complicated freight terminals, has no switching nor interchange delays, is free of the headache of passenger rail agreements, and is even unencumbered by Federal Railroad Administration oversight.

The train runs between the mine and the Alicia Dock facility eight times on a good day. It is run by a single operator, and upon reaching the mine they exit the locomotive and use the Locotrol remote pack to spot the first car underneath the loading chute before climbing up to the loader control room. They operate both the loader and the train and ensure that the cars are loaded uniformly (additionally, they're required to clean up any spills that might occur). It takes roughly 45 minutes to load the train. What was once the trailing DPU is then reconfigured as the lead locomotive and the loaded train departs the mine, bound for the Alicia Dock unloader. It takes a little under an hour for the train to travel the 17 miles of track as it twists and turns through the remote Pennsylvania countryside. A number of bridges, tunnels, and several large cuts keep the grade to a minimum, and there are no public grade crossings at all along the line. The train slows as it nears the dock, passing a small mechanical shop (the railroad performs all car and locomotive maintenance at this facility) and sanding tower before approaching the dump house.

Unloading the train requires a bit of a logistical dance; there is no ground storage at the dock and the silo only holds about a train and a half of coal, which means that unloading is dictated by the availability of barges. Upon reaching the dump house, the operator disembarks from the locomotive cab and resumes remote control of the consist. The operator controls both the movement of the train and the unloading of each car, just as they did during the loading. It takes roughly 45 minutes to empty the train and load the barges, which are shipped downriver until the coal arrives either at the end customer or at a transload facility, where it is transferred from the barges and back onto a train. Once the train is empty, the operator climbs aboard the DPU and reconfigures it as the lead engine before returning to the mine to repeat the process all over again.

The remaining shortlines are truthfully too numerous to list; one could write a book devoted solely to the shortlines around the greater Pittsburgh area. There are a myriad of interchanges and connecting railroads that both originate and terminate rail cars and operate as "feeders" for the larger railroads like Norfolk Southern and CSX. These shortlines are vital to the state's freight infrastructure, and are the reason that Pennsylvania ranks first in the country in the number of operating railroads.

While not technically in Pennsylvania, to tell the full story of the Bessemer Subdivision you must begin in Conneaut, OH. The Bessemer & Lake Erie Railroad was founded by Andrew Carnegie, built to supply his steel mills in Pittsburgh with the raw materials that they required. Nearly 130 years later, this dock is still in operation, with bulk ore carriers like the Great Republic unloading several times a week.

In 2004, Canadian National purchased the BLE and took over daily operations. The iconic Bessemer-orange tunnel motors were eventually repainted and then later replaced by CN SD70-Ms, seen here running long-hood forward (the lead unit is backwards and running in reverse) and leading an ore train across the Allegheny River.

Though CN has taken over the operation of this beloved route, you'll be reminded of this railroad's heritage at every bridge and underpass the Bessemer Line traverses.

A CN SD70-M2 reverses through North Bessemer Yard after tying down the iron-ore loads that they brought down from Conneaut. This engine will couple to the end of the empty ore cars for their return journey. CN runs one ore train daily, the empties typically depart North Bessemer Yard before noon.

The train of empty ore cars accelerates from a stop and slowly rolls out of the yard and back out onto the mainline. Later in the morning, the Union Railroad will arrive at North Bessemer Yard to collect the iron ore loads and drop them off at the blast furnaces.

If the returning empty cars are not delivered to North Bessemer Yard in time for the trip to Conneaut, the engines will depart without them. The lead engines will couple to the DPU, and they will depart north on the Bessemer Subdivision as a light power move.

The Union Railroad serves the facilities that make up the United States Steel Mon Valley Works, the USS Edgar Thomson Steel Works (pictured here with a trio of URR SW1500 switchers backing a train down the ramp and into the mill), the USS Irvin Works, and the USS Clairton Works.

A five-pack of EMD switchers reverse a string of loaded coke cars down into Dexter Yard. Coke is an essential part of the steelmaking process, and it is created locally at the USS Clairton Works through a process called "coking" (where coal is baked at very high temperatures in a "coking oven"). It will ultimately end up fueling the blast furnaces at Edgar Thomson Works.

Two URR trains pass each other, their EMD switchers reverberating throughout the Turtle Creek Valley. The train in the foreground is returning empty coke cars to USS Clairton Works, while the units in the background reverse a cut of scrap metal cars down the ramp and into the mill.

A trio of Union switchers back their cut of scrap-metal-filled gondolas down the ramp and into the yard at Edgar Thomson. This scrap is recycled and made into new steel in the facility's blast furnaces.

After turning around on the wye, a URR engineer throttles up his four EMD switchers and begins the 8-mile journey back to the North Bessemer Yard (where the empty cars will be picked up the following morning by CN and returned to Conneaut for a fresh load of iron ore).

URR trains that travel to North Bessemer must cross through East Pittsburgh and traverse an elevated mainline through the town. One of the benefits of elevating the tracks in this manner is limiting the number of grade crossings through a town.

The Wheeling and Lake Erie Railway operates a fleet of old EMD locomotives (such as these SD40-3s), a number of which are painted in a livery that is an homage to the famed Denver & Rio Grande Railroad. As such, they are a railfan favorite.

The Pittsburgh and Ohio Central Railroad operates out of McKees Rocks, PA, on the former PRR Chartiers Branch. A member of the Genesee & Wyoming railroad holding company, the POHC engines are adorned with their highly visible orange livery.

2161
2161

The Allegheny Valley Railroad (AVR) runs a daily train over to the NS Island Avenue Yard. The AVR is a Class III railroad that connects their customers with NS/CSX by interchanging with the larger Class I railroads. A NS local train rolls down the Conemaugh Line in a rare westward move, past the stopped AVR train.

Opposite page: A POHC GP38-2 is parked underneath the sanding tower at the railroad's service area. Locomotives have utilized sand since the early days of the steam era to increase traction and prevent wheel slip, and modern diesel locomotives are no different.

An AVR SD60M rumbles through "the Trench" and crosses over from Main 4 to Main 3 as it approaches the Island Avenue Yard. This daily train will drop its cars for NS in the yard, then collect a cut of cars that they will bring with them back to the Glenwood Yard (AVR's base of operations).

The engineer of these AVR SD60s applies the air brakes as the manifest train emerges from Panther Hollow and nears Glenwood Yard. The Cathedral of Learning stands in the background, towering over the University of Pittsburgh campus.

Once the cars from Island Avenue Yard arrive in Glenwood Yard, the crew immediately starts switching them in the classification yard according to their ultimate destination. The AVR has a transload facility in Glenwood to transfer frac sand to trucks, as well as a gantry crane that's used to transfer a wide range of commodities from rail to truck (and vice versa).

A four-pack of SD60s traverses the 33rd Street Bridge on the AVR P&W Subdivision through Lawrenceville, PA. The diverging track connects with the AVR Allegheny Subdivision, which runs parallel to the Allegheny River past Verona, Oakmont, and on through to New Kensington.

The lead locomotives that just pulled this coal train from Glenwood Yard on through to Evans City, PA, uncouple from their consist after the conductor sets the required number of handbrakes to tie the train down. A combination of high natural gas prices and low stockpiles at power plants resulted in a short-lived coal traffic boom in the summer of 2022. This resulted in the AVR running coal trains up the P&W Subdivision, where they would interchange the trains with the BPRR (who would then take the train to its final destination).

A quartet of SD60s cruise through Mars, PA, after interchanging another coal train with the BPRR. The red caboose is a former B&O relic that is displayed by the Mars Area History and Landmarks Society.

The Buffalo & Pittsburgh Railroad operates a small yard and locomotive shop in Butler, PA. The BPRR interchanges with CN here; the CN Bessemer Subdivision runs through the Connoquenessing Creek valley and alongside these tracks.

The BPRR is a member of the Genesee & Wyoming railroad holding company (like the POHC). They operate a fleet of older EMD locomotives such as this GP40-2, that are for the most part painted with the iconic orange livery.

A beaten-up Road Slug sits outside the locomotive shops, awaiting repairs. A Road Slug is a locomotive that does not contain an engine (the missing weight is offset with ballast). With no prime mover, these units draw their power from a mother engine and provide additional tractive effort and braking action with no additional fuel penalties.

The nightly BPRR train to CSX's New Castle Yard runs alongside Connoquenessing Creek as it approaches Harmony, PA. The P&W Subdivision parallels this waterway through Zelienople and Ellwood City before reaching the Beaver River and turning north towards the P&W Junction.

The handbrakes are set as the crew walks back and shuts down a pair of BPRR SD60Ms and a SD40-2 on the north end of CSX's New Castle Yard. The BPRR will occasionally stage power here in New Castle.

Having just serviced Austin's Bleach in Valencia, PA, a trio of BPRR engines cruise past the historic B&O Mars Station as they return to Butler. The Mars Station is open every Friday in the summer and offers rides for children on their miniature railway.

A BPRR crew picks up a cut of cars left behind by the AVR earlier in the day, adding them to their train before continuing onward to Butler. There were several rounds of intense storms the day before, which resulted in Breakneck Creek flooding, but fortunately it did not rise over the top of the right-of-way.

The Cumberland Mine Prep Plant is tucked away in the hills of Kirby, PA. This private carrier mining railroad is unencumbered by Federal Railroad Administration oversight, which affords them some operational flexibility. Of note, this train is driven by a single operator. They will disembark at the loader's control room and remotely operate the train while simultaneously filling the empty cars with coal.

Once loaded, the operator climbs aboard the eastern engine (this coal train is bookended with a single SD38-2 on each end) and departs for the 17-mile journey to the Alicia Dock. Seen here crossing Bridge 4 (passing above the aptly named "White Covered Bridge"), it will take this train under an hour to make the trip from mine to dock.

Upon reaching the dock, the train is unloaded directly onto waiting barges. The operator will disembark at the unloader, resume remote operation of the consist, and operate the unloader as they dump each carload of coal. Once the entire train is unloaded, the operator will board the DPU and reconfigure it as the lead engine for the trip back to the mine. All engines face east (and cannot be turned around), so the return trip is run long-hood forward.

The Cumberland Mine's Alicia Dock operates around the clock, transferring coal from train to barge. The silo can only hold one-and-a-half trainloads worth of coal, so unloading is dependent on barge availability.